HAL•LEONARD

INSTRUMENTAL PLAY-ALONG

AUDIO ACCESS INCLUDED

PLAYBACK+
Speed • Pitch • Balance • Loop

Flute

Movie and TV Music

Audio Arrangements by Peter Deneff

To access audio visit:
www.halleonard.com/mylibrary

Enter Code
6273-9018-1810-4146

ISBN 978-1-5400-2062-8

Visit Hal Leonard Online at
www.halleonard.com

Contact Us:
Hal Leonard
7777 West Bluemound Road
Milwaukee, WI 53213
Email: info@halleonard.com

In Europe contact:
Hal Leonard Europe Limited
Distribution Centre, Newmarket Road
Bury St Edmunds, Suffolk, IP33 3YB
Email: info@halleonardeurope.com

In Australia contact:
Hal Leonard Australia Pty. Ltd.
4 Lentara Court
Cheltenham, Victoria, 3192 Australia
Email: info@halleonard.com.au

THE AVENGERS
from THE AVENGERS

Composed by
ALAN SILVESTRI

FLUTE

CAPTAIN AMERICA MARCH
from CAPTAIN AMERICA

By ALAN SILVESTRI

Flute

DOCTOR WHO XI

FLUTE

By MURRAY GOLD

DOWNTON ABBEY
(Theme)

Flute

Music by JOHN LUNN

GAME OF THRONES

Theme from the HBO Series GAME OF THRONES

FLUTE

By RAMIN DJAWADI

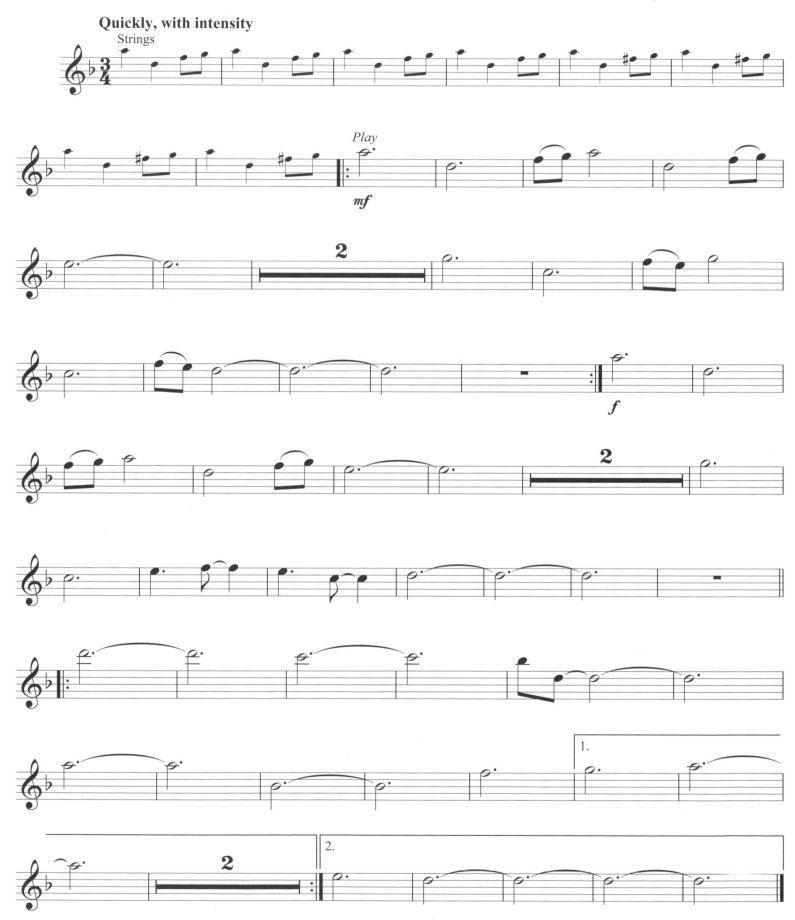

GUARDIANS OF THE GALAXY

from GUARDIANS OF THE GALAXY

Flute

Composed by TYLER BATES,
DIETER HARTMANN, TIMOTHY WILLIAMS
and KURT OLDMAN

HAWAII FIVE-O THEME

from the Television Series

Flute

By MORT STEVENS

MARRIED LIFE

from UP

FLUTE

By MICHAEL GIACCHINO

OUTLANDER THEME
(The Skye Boat Song)

FLUTE

Traditional Music
Arranged by BEAR McCREARY

PROLOGUE AND PROLOGUE PART 2

from BEAUTY AND THE BEAST

Flute

REY'S THEME

from STAR WARS: THE FORCE AWAKENS

FLUTE

Music by JOHN WILLIAMS

THEME FROM THE X-FILES

from the Twentieth Century Fox Television Series THE X-FILES

FLUTE

By MARK SNOW

TEST DRIVE

from the Motion Picture HOW TO TRAIN YOUR DRAGON

FLUTE

By JOHN POWELL